Punny Jokes

Joe King

Abdo Kids Junior
is an Imprint of Abdo Kids
abdobooks.com

abdobooks.com

Published by Abdo Kids, a division of ABDO, P.O. Box 398166, Minneapolis, Minnesota 55439.
Copyright © 2022 by Abdo Consulting Group, Inc. International copyrights reserved in all countries.
No part of this book may be reproduced in any form without written permission from the publisher.
Abdo Kids Junior™ is a trademark and logo of Abdo Kids.

Printed in the United States of America, North Mankato, Minnesota.

102021

012022

Photo Credits: Shutterstock

Production Contributors: Teddy Borth, Jennie Forsberg, Grace Hansen

Design Contributors: Candice Keimig, Pakou Moua

Library of Congress Control Number: 2021940303
Publisher's Cataloging-in-Publication Data

Names: King, Joe, author.
Title: Punny jokes / by Joe King
Description: Minneapolis, Minnesota : Abdo Kids, 2022 | Series: Abdo kids jokes | Includes online resource.
Identifiers: ISBN 9781098209193 (lib. bdg.) | ISBN 9781644946336 (pbk.) | ISBN 9781098209896 (ebook)
    | ISBN 9781098260255 (Read-to-Me ebook)
Subjects: LCSH: Jokes--Juvenile literature. | Wit and humor--Juvenile literature. | Puns and punning--
    Juvenile literature.
Classification: DDC 818.602--dc23

Table of Contents

Punny Jokes

Why did the bird go to
the hospital?

Because it needed some tweetment.

What time do ducks
wake up?

At the quack of dawn!

4

Who stole the soap from the bathtub?
A robber ducky!
HAH!
you quack me up!

What do you call a big pile
of cats?

A meow-tain.

Did you hear the joke about
the little mountain?

It's hill-arious!

ODOR!
ME?
What did the judge say when a skunk walked in?
"Odor in the court!"

Why did the clock get shushed by the librarian?

It was tocking too loud.

What building in New York has the most **stories**?

The public library!

I'm reading a great book about anti-**gravity**.
It's impossible to put down!
BYE!
HEE! HEE!
9

Why did the banana go
to the doctor?

It wasn't peeling well.

Where did the spaghetti and
red sauce go to dance?

The meatball.

What kind of key opens
a banana?

A mon-key!

THANKS
A BUNCH!

YUM!

11

What did the cupcake
say to the frosting?

"I'd be muffin without you!"

What do you call a
fake noodle?

An impasta!

What did the baby corn ask the mama corn?
Where's my pop corn?
POP
POP
POP
POP
POP
That joke was corny...
POPCORN
13

We dressed up as almonds
for Halloween.

Everyone thought we were nuts!

What do you call a dinosaur
that never gives up?

A try-try-try-ceratops!

RAWW HA! HA!
Where does a T. Rex shop?
At the dinostore.
15

I can't believe I got fired from the calendar factory...

All I did was take a day off!

I'm an archaeologist.

My career is in ruins.

Why did the scarecrow win an award?
Because he was outstanding in his field.
CLAP! CLAP!
This joke should win an award!
17

What do astronauts do before a party in space?

They planet!

Did you hear about the guy whose whole left side was cut off?

He's all right now.

How do you talk to
a giant?
Use big words!
HA! HA!
HA! HA!
HA!

How do we know the ocean

is friendly?

It waves!

Why did everyone want to

be around the volcano?

It was just so lava-ble.

What kind of tree fits in your hand?
A palm tree.
TALK TO THE PALM!
21

Joke-Telling Tips!

- Know your audience

- Timing is everything

- Confidence is key

- Go out on a high note!

Glossary

pun

a joke using a word that sounds like a different word or has another meaning. Examples from this book are "lavable" (loveable) and "peeling" (feeling).

gravity

the force by which all objects in the universe are attracted to each other.

story

one level of a building.

Index

Visit **abdokids.com** to access crafts, games, videos, and more!